Readers' Theater: How to Put on a Production

Medals and Memorials

A Readers' Theater Script and Guide

Looking Glass Library

An Imprint of Magic Wagon
abdopublishing.com

By Nancy K. Wallace   Illustrated by Nina Mata

In memory of Sgt. Leslie H. Sabo Jr., a friend and hometown hero. —NKW
To my parents, my loving husband Aaron & my darling Aria. —NM

abdopublishing.com

Published by Magic Wagon, a division of ABDO, PO Box 398166, Minneapolis, Minnesota 55439.
Copyright © 2016 by Abdo Consulting Group, Inc. International copyrights reserved in all countries. No part of this book may be reproduced in any form without written permission from the publisher. Looking Glass Library™ is a trademark and logo of Magic Wagon.

Printed in the United States of America, North Mankato, Minnesota.
042015
092015

THIS BOOK CONTAINS
RECYCLED MATERIALS

Written by Nancy K. Wallace
Illustrations by Nina Mata
Edited by Heidi M.D. Elston, Megan M. Gunderson & Bridget O'Brien
Designed by Laura Mitchell

Library of Congress Cataloging-in-Publication Data

Wallace, Nancy K.
  Medals and memorials : a readers' theater script and guide / by Nancy K. Wallace ; illustrated by Nina Mata.
     pages cm. -- (Readers' theater: how to put on a production set 2)
  ISBN 978-1-62402-115-2
1. Memorial Day--Juvenile drama. 2. Theater--Production and direction--Juvenile literature. 3. Readers' theater--Juvenile literature. I. Mata, Nina, 1981- illustrator. II. Title.
  PS3623.A4436M43 2015
  812'.6--dc23
                                    2014050080

Table of Contents

Celebrate with a Play!

Everyone loves holidays! Some schools and libraries hold programs or assemblies to commemorate special occasions. This series offers fun plays to help celebrate six different holidays at your school or library. You can even sell tickets and use your play as a fund-raiser.

Readers' theater can be done very simply. The performers sit on stools or chairs onstage. They don't have to memorize their lines. They just read them.

Adapted readers' theater looks more like a regular play. The stage includes scenery and props. The performers wear makeup and costumes. They move around to show the action. But, they still carry their scripts.

Readers' theater scripts can also be used for puppet shows. The performers stand behind a curtain, move the puppets, and read their scripts.

Find a place large enough to put on a play. An auditorium with a stage is ideal. A classroom will work, too. Choose a date and ask permission to use the space. Advertise your play with posters and flyers. Place them around your school and community. Tell your friends and family. Everyone enjoys watching a fun performance!

Tickets and Playbills

Tickets and playbills can be handwritten or designed on a computer. Be sure tickets include the title of the play. They should list the date, time, and location of the performance.

A playbill is a printed program. The front of a playbill has the title of the play, the date, and the time. The cast and crew are listed inside. Be sure to have enough playbills for the audience and cast. Pass them out at the door as the audience enters.

The Crew

Next, a crew is needed. The show can't go on without these important people! Some jobs can be combined for a small show.

Director — organizes everyone and everything in the show.

Costume Designer — designs and borrows or makes all the costumes.

Stage Manager — makes sure everything runs smoothly.

Lighting Designer — runs spotlights and other lighting.

Set Designer — plans and makes scenery.

Prop Manager — finds, makes, and keeps track of props.

Special Effects Crew — takes care of sound and other special effects.

Sets

At a readers' theater production, the performers can sit on stools at the front of the room. An adapted readers' theater production or full play will require sets and props. A set is the background that creates the setting for each scene. A prop is an item the actors use onstage.

Scene 1 should look like a front porch. Borrow a lawn chair and use some real or artificial flowers in pots. For the background, paint sheets of cardboard to look like a house with windows and a door. Cardboard trees will help set the scene, too.

Scene 2 takes place in Katie's kitchen. This scene requires a table and a chair or stool. For the background, a stove or sink can be painted on cardboard.

Scene 3 is in Mrs. Cortez's living room. Use two comfortable chairs, a side table, and a coffee table. Borrow a wheelchair and be sure to leave room for it on the set. Make the set feel like a home using wallpaper-covered cardboard or an area rug.

Scene 4 takes place in front of the curtain or on an empty stage. Katie, R.J., and Reece can be wearing their backpacks.

Scene 5 takes place outside. Use the cardboard trees from scene 1 as well as a tombstone.

Props

- 1 sheet of paper
- Briefcase
- Lawn chair
- 4 pots of artificial flowers (2 should be roses)

- Bowl or container of icing with spoon
- Foil-covered plate
- Plate of real brownies
- Butter knife

- Wheelchair
- Framed picture of a young soldier
- Set of silverware
- 3 backpacks

The Cast

Decide who will play each part. Each person in the cast will need a script. All of the performers should practice their lines. Reading lines aloud over and over will help the performers learn them. *Medals and Memorials* needs the following cast:

Katie Oliver — a third grader

Reece — Katie's friend

R.J. — Katie's friend

Mr. Oliver — Katie's dad

Mrs. Oliver — Katie's mom

Mrs. Cortez — Katie's elderly neighbor

Mrs. Custer — Katie's teacher

Class — the students in Katie's class

Makeup and Costumes

Makeup artists have a big job! Every cast member wears makeup. And, stage makeup needs to be brighter and heavier than regular makeup. Buy several basic shades of mascara, foundation, blush, and lipstick. Apply with a new cotton ball or swab for each cast member to avoid spreading germs.

Costume designers set the scene just as much as set designers. They borrow costumes or adapt old clothing for each character. Ask adults for help finding and sewing costumes.

Most of the performers in this play can wear regular clothes they would wear to school. There are a few exceptions.

Mrs. Cortez should wear a white wig and keep a handkerchief in one pocket. The makeup designer can carefully apply "wrinkles" using an eyebrow pencil.

Mr. Oliver should wear a shirt and tie. Give him a fake mustache!

Mrs. Custer should wear a sweater and skirt or a dress.

Rehearsals and Stage Directions

After you decide to put on a play, it is important to set up a rehearsal schedule. Choose a time everyone can attend, such as after school or on weekends. Try to have at least five rehearsals before the performance.

Everyone should practice together as a team, even though individual actors will be reading their own scripts. This will help the play sound like a conversation, instead of separate lines. Onstage, actors should act like their characters even when they aren't speaking.

In the script, stage directions are in parentheses. They are given from the performer's point of view, not the audience's. Actors face the audience when performing, so left is on their left and right is on their right.

Some theater terms may be unfamiliar:

Curtains — the main curtain at the front of the stage.

House — the area in which the audience sits.

Wings — the part of the stage on either side that the audience can't see.

Downstage

Stage
Left

Center Stage

Stage
Right

Left Wing

Upstage

Right Wing

Script: Medals and Memorials
Scene 1: Katie's Front Porch

(Katie, Reece, and R.J. sit on Katie's front porch. Use a lawn chair and potted plants to set the stage. Reece is making a paper airplane.)

Katie: Did you decide what you're going to do for your project?

Reece: No, did you?

Katie: *(Throwing up her hands.)* I don't even have any ideas!

R.J.: I think maybe I'll write about tanks.

Reece: Or airplanes! *(Reece makes a whining noise and launches a paper airplane.)*

(Katie's father, Mr. Oliver, enters from upstage right, carrying a briefcase.)

Mr. Oliver: Hey, buddy! Don't launch air strikes on my wife's plants!

R.J.: It's just a paper airplane, Mr. Oliver.

Mr. Oliver: That's a relief!

Katie: Hi, Dad!

Mr. Oliver: Hi, kiddo! It's such a beautiful day! What's the matter? You all look so glum!

Katie: Mrs. Custer asked us to do Memorial Day projects . . .

Reece: *(Interrupting.)* . . . but we don't have any ideas.

Mr. Oliver: Didn't you go to the school library?

Katie: *Everyone* did! Everyone is just writing a report. *(Katie counts to three on her fingers as she speaks.)* Memorial Day used to be called Decoration Day because people decorated graves with flowers. It honors people who died in wars. It's the last Monday in May.

Mr. Oliver: Why don't you want to write about that, too?

Reece: It's kind of boring.

Mr. Oliver: Have you kids ever thought about what the holiday means to you personally?

R.J.: *(Enthusiastically.)* We get a day off school!

Reece: And we usually have a picnic.

Katie: You and Mom and I always go to the parade.

Mr. Oliver: You're thinking about ways that people spend Memorial Day, but not how they feel about it. Maybe you need to do some more research. You could talk to someone who actually fought in a war or had a family member who did.

Reece: I think my uncle Ryan used to be a marine. He lives in California.

Mr. Oliver: Why don't you ask your mom if you can call him? I'm sure he could tell you something more personal to include in your project.

R.J.: My aunt Kathy is in Afghanistan right now!

Mr. Oliver: When is your project due?

R.J.: Next week.

Mr. Oliver: You could probably e-mail her. Or just talk to her family. Ask what Memorial Day means to them.

(Reece and R.J. jump up.)

Reece: Thanks, Mr. Oliver!

R.J.: Yeah, thanks! You have great ideas! See you later, Katie!

(Reece and R.J. exit stage right.)

Mr. Oliver: Bye, boys!

Katie: *(In a disgusted voice.)* Yeah, thanks a bunch. Now everyone has an idea but me!

Mr. Oliver: *(Exiting stage left.)* Don't worry! I'm sure we can think of something great.

Scene 2: The Kitchen at Katie's House

(Set the scene with a kitchen table and a stool to the right. Put a bowl of icing with a spoon, a butter knife, and a plate covered with aluminum foil on the table. Add a plate of real brownies. Mrs. Oliver stands at the table stirring the icing. Katie enters from stage left and sits down on the stool, facing stage right.)

Mrs. Oliver: There you are! Could you help me for a few minutes?

Katie: Sure.

Mrs. Oliver: *(Pushing the foil-covered plate toward Katie.)* I made dinner for our neighbor, Mrs. Cortez. Could you take it over to her? I thought maybe you could cheer her up.

Katie: Sure. I noticed there are a lot of weeds around her roses when I was on our porch. Maybe I can help her with her garden, too.

Mrs. Oliver: That would be very nice, Katie! She's having a lot of trouble getting around since her surgery.

Katie: I'll ask her today. She can just sit on the porch and tell me what to do.

Mrs. Oliver: I'm sure she'll appreciate that. She loves those roses.

Katie: I can go over again tomorrow after school. I'm sure Reece and R.J. will help me.

Mrs. Oliver: Where are the boys? I thought you three were going to work on your Memorial Day projects this afternoon.

Katie: Dad gave them both great ideas for their projects. They went home to work on them.

Mrs. Oliver: Did he give you an idea, too?

Katie: No, not really. Do we have any soldiers in our family?

Mrs. Oliver: Your great-grandfather was in the navy. He fought in World War II, but I don't know where. I have some pictures of him in his uniform that I can try to find for you.

Katie: Okay, thanks! At least it's a start.

Mrs. Oliver: These brownies are for dessert. Would you like to ice them for me?

Katie: *(Taking the icing and the butter knife.)* I'd love to! It looks like the boys missed out. Now there'll be more brownies for us! These look yummy!

Scene 3: Mrs. Cortez's House

(Set two chairs with a coffee table between them at center stage. Put a lamp and a picture on a table at stage left. Mrs. Cortez is stage left, sitting in her wheelchair.)

Katie: *(Knocks and then speaks from the wings.)* Mrs. Cortez? It's Katie Oliver from next door.

Mrs. Cortez: Just a minute, Katie! *(She uses her wheelchair to cross the room and pretends to open the door.)*

Katie: *(Enters from stage right.)* Hi, Mrs. Cortez. My mom sent you some dinner.

Mrs. Cortez: That was very nice of her! Just put it on the table here, honey. *(She goes back to sit near the table.)*

Katie: And there are brownies for dessert!

Mrs. Cortez: Brownies are my favorite! They look delicious.

Katie: *(Puts the food on the table.)* How are you feeling?

Mrs. Cortez: Much better, dear. Thank you for asking.

Katie: This is hot. Do you want me to get you some silverware so you can eat it now?

Mrs. Cortez: Thank you! The kitchen is right through there. *(Points to stage left.)*

(Katie exits stage left and returns with a spoon, a knife, and a fork.)

Mrs. Cortez: *(Begins to speak as Katie returns.)* Do you have time to sit down for a minute? I've been eating my dinner in front of the TV since I came home from the hospital. It would be nice to have someone to talk to. *(She begins to take the foil from the plate.)*

Katie: *(Sits down.)* Sure! I wanted to talk to you about your garden anyway.

Mrs. Cortez: *(Sounding sad.)* Oh, my poor roses! They are all full of weeds. I'm just not able to go out and take care of them right now.

Katie: I thought maybe my friends and I could weed them for you.

Mrs. Cortez: Oh, Katie! That would be wonderful!

Katie: I could start today if you show me what to do.

Mrs. Cortez: Thank you! Those roses are very important to me. My son gave them to me. There's a picture of him over there.

(Katie stands up, walks over to the table, and picks up a picture of a young man in uniform.)

Katie: *(Sounding excited.)* Mrs. Cortez, was your son a soldier?

Mrs. Cortez: Yes, he was killed in Vietnam.

Katie: *(Sounding embarrassed.)* I'm so sorry. I didn't know that.

Mrs. Cortez: It was a long time ago, honey.

Katie: And he gave you those roses?

Mrs. Cortez: *(Smiling.)* Yes. Every year for Mother's Day he would buy me a new rosebush.

Katie: Wow! Those rosebushes must be very old!

Mrs. Cortez: *(Laughing.)* Some of them have died over the years, but many of them are still alive. That's why they're so important to me. They remind me of John every time I see them.

Katie: Don't worry! I'll help you take care of them.

Mrs. Cortez: Thank you. John was a good son and a good soldier. He got the Medal of Honor.

Katie: *(Puts the picture down.)* Your son got the Medal of Honor? Wow, that sounds important!

Mrs. Cortez: The Medal of Honor is given to someone who shows unusual valor in combat.

Katie: I don't know what that means.

Mrs. Cortez: *Valor* means "bravery" or "courage," Katie.

Katie: What did your son do?

Mrs. Cortez: John died saving the lives of five other soldiers. *(Mrs. Cortez pulls out a handkerchief and wipes her eyes.)*

Katie: Oh, Mrs. Cortez, I am so sorry! My mom sent me over here to cheer you up and I made you cry!

Mrs. Cortez: It's all right, Katie. I've just been thinking about John all day. I don't want him to be forgotten after I'm gone. On Memorial Day, I always take a bouquet of roses to the cemetery.

Katie: To decorate John's grave?

Mrs. Cortez: Yes, it's one of the special ways I remember him. *(She pauses.)* But I'm not sure if I'll be able to go this year.

Katie: Don't worry, Mrs. Cortez. I have an awesome idea!

Scene 4: Outside the School

(This scene takes place in front of the curtain. No scenery is needed. The stage crew can set up quietly for scene 5 behind the curtain. If there is no curtain, set up for scene 5 after scene 4.)

(Katie enters from stage right. Reece enters from stage left. They are wearing or carrying backpacks.)

Katie: Hi, Reece!

Reece: *(Gloomily.)* Hi, Katie.

Katie: What's the matter?

Reece: I don't have a project for Memorial Day.

Katie: I thought you were going to call your uncle Ryan.

(R.J. walks in from stage left while the conversation is going on.)

Reece: I did. I talked to my aunt Judy. My uncle went camping in the mountains for two weeks. He's out of cell phone range.

R.J.: I have a problem, too! My aunt Kathy is out on some secret mission in Afghanistan.

Reece: Wow! She's on a secret mission?

R.J.: Well, her family said she was out on "maneuvers," but I think it's probably a secret mission, don't you?

Reece: Yeah!

Katie: *(Shakes her head.)* You guys are funny.

R.J.: Either way, she hasn't been answering e-mails for the last week. How's your project going, Katie? Did you think of something to do?

Katie: Yes, I did! And if it's okay with Mrs. Custer, I think you two could help.

Reece: Really? It would be awesome if we could all do a project together!

R.J.: *(Gives Katie a high five.)* Thanks, Katie!

Katie: Come on! Let's go ask Mrs. Custer right now.

(All three students exit stage left.)

Scene 5: Saint Mark's Cemetery

(Place a foam or cardboard tombstone and two cardboard trees at upstage center. Katie, Reece, R.J., Mrs. Custer, and Mrs. Cortez, in her wheelchair, are at center stage. The rest of the class sits stage right and stage left in a semicircle.)

Mrs. Custer: Well, class, as part of their Memorial Day project, Katie, Reece, and R.J. arranged this field trip to Saint Mark's Cemetery. I'll let Katie tell you why we are here.

(Reece and R.J. each carry a pot of artificial roses. They stand near Katie.)

Katie: When I was trying to find something to do my project on, I didn't know what to do. The things I read at the library didn't sound very exciting to me. Then, my mom asked me to take dinner to my neighbor. *(Katie turns to smile at Mrs. Cortez.)* This is Mrs. Cortez.

(Everyone claps.)

Mrs. Cortez: Hello, class.

Katie: I found out that Mrs. Cortez had a son named John. He was a sergeant during the Vietnam War. He died on Mother's Day in 1970 while saving five other soldiers.

(Students gasp and begin to whisper.)

Mrs. Custer: Quiet down, everyone! Let's be good listeners.

Katie: *(Turning to point to the tombstone.)* John Cortez is buried here in Saint Mark's Cemetery. Memorial Day is about remembering the soldiers who have died protecting us. It is important that we don't forget them. So I asked Mrs. Cortez to tell us a little bit about her son so we could all get to know him better.

Reece: John was a hero, but he was a lot like us, too. John went to our school when he was little. He loved math and hated English class.

(Everyone laughs.)

Reece: He fell off a horse when he was ten. He loved spaghetti and chocolate ice cream. He played football in high school. He broke his arm skiing. John went to college for two years before he joined the military. He fell in love and got married. A month later, he left for Vietnam. John was only twenty-two years old when he died.

R.J.: Memorial Day is about remembering all the men and women who have died for our country. Years ago, people went to cemeteries on Memorial Day to plant flowers on the graves of servicemen and servicewomen. They brought picnic lunches. They told stories about these men and women so that their courage wouldn't be forgotten.

Katie: Every year on Mother's Day, John Cortez gave his mother a rosebush. Every Memorial Day since he died, she has brought roses to put on his grave.

Mrs. Cortez: This year, I wasn't sure I would make it to the cemetery with any roses for my John. Thank you so much, Katie, Reece, and R.J., for making it possible!

Mrs. Custer: Mrs. Cortez, this has been a special project for Katie, Reece, and R.J. And it has been a special day for our class. After learning John's story today, I know he won't ever be forgotten!

(Class stands up and cheers and claps.)

Mrs. Cortez: *(Wipes her eyes with her handkerchief.)* This means so much to me, class. Thank you!

Katie: This is our special thank you to our own hometown hero!

(Everyone claps.)

The End

Adapting Readers' Theater Scripts

Readers' theater can be done very simply. Performers just read their lines from scripts. They don't have to memorize them! And, they don't have to move around. The performers sit on chairs or stools while reading their parts.

Adapted Readers' Theater: This looks more like a regular play. The performers wear makeup and costumes. The stage has scenery and props. The cast moves around to show the action. Performers can still read from their scripts.

A Puppet Show: Some schools and libraries have puppet collections. Or students can create puppets. Students make the puppets be the actors. They read their scripts for their puppets.

Teaching Guides

Readers' Theater Teaching Guides are available online at **abdopublishing.com**. Each guide includes printable scripts, reading levels for each character, and additional production tips for each play. Get yours today!

Websites

To learn more about Readers' Theater, visit **booklinks.abdopublishing.com**. These links are routinely monitored and updated to provide the most current information available.